——— ◼ ———

*E*nfolded within the pages of this
book are so many wonderful wishes
and meaningful gifts that I would
love to give to you.

May they brighten and bless all the
seasons of your life.

——— ◼ ———

Endless thanks are given to those who gave me an awareness of the value of the "gifts" contained in this book, and tremendous appreciation is felt for fellow writers whose wisdom fills these pages. This book is dedicated to three special gifts in my life: my wife, Carrie, and my sons, Jordan and Casey.

We wish to thank Susan Polis Schutz for permission to reprint the quote "Go beyond yourself..." in this publication. Copyright © 1976, 1992 by Stephen Schutz and Susan Polis Schutz. All rights reserved.

Excerpt from "Little Gidding" in FOUR QUARTETS, Copyright © 1942 by T. S. Eliot and renewed 1970 by Esme Valerie Eliot, reprinted by permission of Hartcourt, Inc., and Faber and Faber Limited. A careful effort has been made to trace the ownership of selections used in this anthology in order to obtain permission to reprint copyrighted material and give proper credit to the copyright owners. If any error or omission has occurred, it is completely inadvertent, and we would like to make corrections in future editions provided that written notification is made to the publisher.

Library of Congress Catalog Card Number: 99-16855
ISBN: 0-88396-639-5 (trade paper) — ISBN: 0-88396-524-0 (expanded hardcover edition)

Certain trademarks are used under license.

Manufactured in the United States of America.
Second printing of this edition: 2003

Library of Congress Cataloging-in-Publication Data

These are the gifts I'd like to give to you : a sourcebook of joy and
    encouragement / edited by Douglas Pagels.
        p. cm.
 ISBN 0-88396-639-5 (trade paper : alk. paper)
 ISBN 0-88396-524-0 (hardcover : alk. paper)
 1. Joy Quotations, maxims, etc. 2. Encouragement Quotations, maxims, etc. I. Pagels, Douglas.
 PN6084.J65T49 2000
 152.4'2—dc21   99-16855
                                                      CIP

SPS Studios, Inc.
P.O. Box 4549, Boulder, Colorado 80306

These Are the

GIFTS

I'd Like
to Give to You

A Sourcebook of
Joy and Encouragement

Edited by Douglas Pagels

Blue Mountain Press™
SPS Studios, Inc., Boulder, Colorado

Contents

The Gift of...

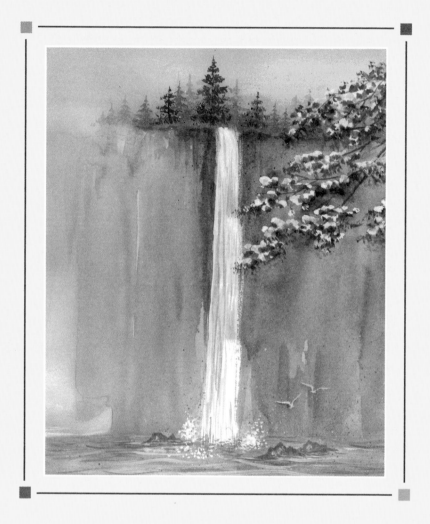

The Gift of Welcoming
the Wonder

I walk the world in wonder.

— Oscar Wilde

Not knowing when the dawn will come,
I open every door.

— Emily Dickinson

And all the windows
of my heart
I open to the day.

— John Greenleaf Whittier

Each day brings with it the miracle of a new
beginning. Many of the moments ahead will
be marvelously disguised as ordinary days,
but each one of us has the chance to make
something extraordinary out of them.

— Douglas Pagels

The Gift of Imagining the Possibilities

The principle business of life
is to enjoy it.

— Samuel Butler

Many of us have road maps we envision for the
course we think our lives should take. It's important
to get headed in the right direction, but don't get
so caught up in the concerns over your destination
that you forget to delight in the scenery of each
new day. Remember that some of the secret joys
of living are not found by rushing from point A
to point B, but by inventing some imaginary letters
along the way.

— Douglas Pagels

The truth is that everything
is a miracle and a wonder.

— Rabbi Barukh

Out of every earth day,
make a little bit of heaven.

— Ella Wheeler Wilcox

The Gift of Some of the Most Wonderful Wisdom of All

It is never
too late
to be
what you
might have been.

— George Eliot

We can bring so many blessings
into our lives just by realizing
that it is *never too late*. Before
you turn the page on this day,
make a pact with yourself to
untie the ribbons and open the
gifts we are given in this life. Do
ordinary things in extraordinary
ways. Have health and hope and
happiness! Live a full life on this
earth, understand your real worth,
and wish on all your stars.

And don't ever forget, for even a day,
how very special
you are.

— Douglas Pagels

The Gift of Letting
Your Creativity Shine

Be creative!
You're the artist here.
You're the one who can
brush away the clouds
and make the sun shine.
Paint your own picture,
choose your own colors.
And forget all that
business about having to
stay between the lines.

— Douglas Pagels

Every artist dips his brush in his soul, and
paints his own nature into his pictures.

— Henry Ward Beecher

Expressing your creativity is done more by the
way you are living than by any other gesture.

— Douglas Pagels

To affect the quality of the day —
that is the highest of the arts.

— Henry David Thoreau

The Gift of Appreciating
Life to the Fullest

I may be uncertain about exactly where
I'm headed, but I am very clear regarding
this: I'm glad I've got a ticket to go on this
magnificent journey.

— Douglas Pagels

There is no cure for birth and death
save to enjoy the interval.

— George Santayana

That it will never come again
Is what makes life so sweet.

— Emily Dickinson

It is a grand thing to live — to open the eyes
in the morning and look out upon the world;
to drink in the pure air and enjoy the sweet
sunshine; to feel the pulse bound and the being
thrill with the consciousness of strength and
power in every nerve. It is a good thing simply
to be alive, and it is a good world to live in,
in spite of the abuse we are fond of giving it.

— Anonymous

The Gift of Asking, Believing, Receiving

I ask not for a lighter burden,
but for broader shoulders.

— Jewish Proverb

Do not pray for easier lives.
Pray to be stronger men. Do
not pray for tasks equal to
your powers. Pray for powers
equal to your tasks! Then the
doing of your work shall be
no miracle, but you shall be
the miracle.

— Phillips Brooks

I ask not for a larger garden,
but for finer seeds.

— Russell Herma Cornwell

Keep on sowing your seed, for you
never know which will grow —
perhaps it all will.

— Ecclesiastes 11:6

The Gift of Gentle Words
in Difficult Times

The mantra to help you make it through:
"Need to, can do. Have to, will do."

— Douglas Pagels

If you can walk, you can dance.
If you can talk, you can sing.

— Zimbabwean Proverb

Although the world is full of suffering,
it is also full of the overcoming of it.

— Helen Keller

When life hands you a lemon,
squeeze it and start a lemonade stand.

— Anonymous

The Gift of Keeping
Worries Away

It is foolish to worry about
anything so temporary as today.

— Anonymous

Worry is like a rocking chair — it will
give you something to do, but it
won't get you anywhere.

— Anonymous

Nothing wastes more energy
than worrying. The longer one
carries a problem, the heavier
it gets. Don't take things too
seriously. Live a life of serenity,
not a life of regrets.

— Douglas Pagels

The words "peace" and "tranquility"
are worth a thousand pieces of gold.

— Chinese Proverb

The Gift of Paying
Attention to the Details

Most of us will never do great things,
but we can do small things in a great way.

— Anonymous

A great artist can paint a great picture
on a small canvas.

— Charles Dudley Warner

Admire your accomplishments.
Large or small, tremendous or
tiny, they contribute to the
well-being of this world. A little
light somewhere makes a brighter
light everywhere. A speck of
sand can turn into a pearl.

— Douglas Pagels

Buried deep in the maze of commonplace,
the pearl of true happiness lies. And he who
rejoices in little things finds the pathway
that leads to the prize.

— Lucy M. Thompson

The Gift of Understanding
What Makes You So Outstanding

People go abroad to wonder at the height of mountains, at the huge waves of the sea, at the long courses of the rivers, at the vast compasses of the ocean... and they pass by themselves without even imagining.

— Augustine of Hippo

What the world is for us
depends on what we are ourselves.

— Lewis G. Janes

Every individual is a marvel of
unknown and unrealized possibilities.

— W. G. Jordon

You're an original, an individual, a masterpiece. Celebrate that; don't let your uniqueness make you shy. Don't be someone other than the wonder you are. Every star is important to the sky.

— Douglas Pagels

What should I be but just what I am?

— Edna St. Vincent Millay

The Gift of Recognizing Opportunity When It Knocks

To improve the golden moment of
opportunity and catch the good that
is within our reach is the great art of life.

— Samuel Johnson

Opportunity seems to have an uncanny habit of favoring
those who have paid the price of years of preparation.

— Anonymous

Opportunities sometimes drop into
people's laps, but not until they get their
laps where opportunities are dropping.

— Mildred Seydell

There is an old saying that opportunity knocks but once;
yet history shows that this is not true. Opportunities for
happiness and progress may come in different forms, but
they are with us daily. If those for which we seek seem
not at hand today, let us not despair. They will come
again and again, hopeful for the day we will be able and
ready to recognize and grasp them.

— Anonymous

The Gift of Honoring That Person in the Mirror

To find yourself, think for yourself.

— Socrates

Until you mean something to yourself,
you can't be important to anyone else.
One must live the good alone-life in order
to grow and develop in one's own way.

— Grace Moore

Everyone sees you as you appear to be;
few realize what you really are.

— Niccolo Machiavelli

Don't ever be your own worst critic. Always try
to be your own best ally. There are times when
it helps to acknowledge that: "I am aware that
I am less than some people prefer me to be, but
most people are unaware that I am so much
more than what they see."

— Douglas Pagels

The Gift of Faith Having a Place in Your Life

As a knot appears unexpectedly in a thread,
so disappointment blocks the smoothness of life.
If a few deft strokes can untangle the skein, life
continues evenly. But if it cannot be corrected,
then it must be quietly woven into the design.
Thus, the finished piece can still be beautiful —
even though not as perfect as planned.

— Anonymous

We sleep, but the loom of life never stops
and the pattern which was weaving when
the sun went down — is weaving when it
comes up tomorrow.

— Henry Ward Beecher

The sunrise never failed us yet.

— Celia Thaxter

For any weaving that needs to
be done, God sends the threads.

— Italian Proverb

The Gift of
a Happy Home

He is happiest, be he king or peasant,
who finds peace in his home.

— Johann Wolfgang von Goethe

I had rather be on my farm than be emperor of the world.

— George Washington

I had rather be shut up in a very modest cottage, with my books, my family and a few old friends... letting the world roll on as it likes, than to occupy the most splendid post which any human power can give.

— Thomas Jefferson

Make two homes for thyself...
One actual home... and another
spiritual home, which thou art
to carry with thee always.

— Saint Catherine of Siena

Home, in one form or another, is the great object of life.

— Josiah Gilbert Holland

The Gift of Guilt-Free Relaxation

Rest is not idleness, and to lie on the grass under the trees on a summer's day, listening to the murmur of water, or watching the clouds float across the sky, is by no means a waste of time.

— John Lubbock

He does not seem to me to be a free man who does not sometimes do nothing.

— Cicero

Lying in bed would be an altogether perfect and supreme experience if only one had a colored pencil long enough to draw on the ceiling.

— G. K. Chesterton

The time you enjoy wasting is not wasted time.

— Bertrand Russell

The Gift of Comprehending
What Others Are Going Through

Be kind. Everyone you meet is fighting a hard battle.

— John Watson

One of the injustices of life is being judged by others, when those judging might be guilty, as well. Don't scrutinize people with a microscope; view them from a comfortable distance. And allow some room for compassion in the space that lies between you.

— Douglas Pagels

Go beyond yourself and reach out to other people with a sincere love, respect, caring, and understanding of their needs.

— Susan Polis Schutz

Resolve to be: tender with the young, compassionate with the aged, sympathetic with the striving, and tolerant of the weak and the wrong. There will be times in your life when you will have been all of these.

— Anonymous

The Gift of Dressing
for Success

Of all the things you wear,
your expression is the most important.

— Anonymous

We must cut our coat according to our cloth,
and adapt ourselves to changing circumstances.

— Dean W. R. Inge

Self-respect is the noblest garment with which
a man may clothe himself, the most elevating
feeling with which the mind can be inspired.

— Samuel Smiles

When one has much to put in them,
a day has a hundred pockets.

— Friedrich Nietzsche

The Gift of Listening
to Your Heart

There are choices ahead which could change your life. Unfortunately, there aren't any crystal balls to provide the answers, telling you where to go or what to do. But it is true that centuries of wisdom have never improved on this advice:

Just listen to your heart.

— Douglas Pagels

We do not know where we are going, but we are on our way.

— Stephen Vincent Benét

Trust your intuition. Its sources spring from deep within the soul.

— Douglas Pagels

Every wakeful step, every mindful act is the direct path to awakening. Wherever you go, there you are.

— Buddha

The Gift of Finding Out
How Much Fun It Can Be

Cheerfulness keeps up a kind of delight
in the mind, and fills it with a steady
and perpetual serenity.

— Joseph Addison

Angels fly because they
take themselves lightly.

— G. K. Chesterton

There aren't many things as therapeutic
as smiles and laughter. Whenever you
look at things in a lighter vein, it shows
that your heart is in the right place.

— Douglas Pagels

Every survival kit should include
a sense of humor.

— Anonymous

The Gift of Getting to Know
Your Fellow Travelers

We must think of life as a journey.... Let us think of ways in which we can make the journey more pleasant for others as well as for ourselves. Let us remember that life's journey is good, it is thrilling, and it can be made beautiful if we do our part.

— Seth Harmon

We desire to be classified according to our exceptional virtues; we are apt to classify others according to their exceptional faults.

— Henry Bates Diamond

Every man is entitled to be valued by his best moment.

— Ralph Waldo Emerson

I am going your way, so let us go hand in hand. You help me and I'll help you. We shall not be here very long... so let us help one another while we may.

— William Morris

The Gift of Being Enthusiastic!

You can do anything
if you have enthusiasm.

— Henry Ford

I am unaware of anything
that has a right
to be called an impossibility.

— Thomas H. Huxley

We act as though comfort and luxury
were the chief requirements of life, when
all that we need to make us really happy
is something to be enthusiastic about.

— Charles Kingsley

Nothing is so contagious as enthusiasm!
It is the genius of sincerity, and truth
accomplishes no victories without it.

— Anonymous

The Gift of a Balance
Between Dollars and Sense

One of the hardest things about making money last — is the ability to make it first.

— Anonymous

Money doesn't make you happy, but it quiets the nerves.

— Sean O'Casey

More people should tell their dollars where to go, rather than asking them where they went.

— Anonymous

It's good to have money and the things that money can buy, but it's good, too, to check up once in a while and be sure you haven't lost the things money can't buy.

— George H. Lorimer

The Gift of Real Accomplishment

If we want to know what happiness is, we must seek it, not as if it were a pot of gold at the end of the rainbow, but among human beings who are living richly and fully the good life. If you observe a really happy man, you will find him building a boat, writing a symphony, educating his children, growing double dahlias in his garden. He will not be searching for happiness... he will have become aware that he is happy in the course of living twenty-four crowded hours in the day.

— W. Beran Wolfe

Remember that there is one thing
better than making a living —
making a life.

— Anonymous

Sometimes it's important to work for that pot of gold. But other times it's essential to take time off and to make sure that your most important decision in the day simply consists of choosing which color to slide down on the rainbow.

— Douglas Pagels

The Gift of Helping Those Around You

Ten rules for getting rid of the blues:
Go out and do something nice for
someone else, then repeat it nine times.

— Anonymous

Life is like a game of tennis: the
player who serves well seldom loses.

— Anonymous

He who, forgetting self, makes the object of
his life service, helpfulness, and kindness to
others, finds his whole nature growing and
expanding, himself becoming large-hearted,
magnanimous, kind, sympathetic, joyous, and
happy; his life becoming rich and beautiful.

— Ralph Waldo Trine

Helping someone else
is the secret of happiness.

— Booker T. Washington

The Gift of
Enjoying It All

There is no season such delight can bring
as summer, autumn, winter, and the spring.

— William Browne

Talk with the year which is coming as with a friend
who is crossing your threshold to bring you gifts.
Say, I welcome you. Let me come close to you; let
me walk beside you and listen to all the secrets
which you keep in your great soul for my sharing...

If I breathe in your pure airs, if I live according to
those natural laws which govern you, if I accept the
spring, the summer, the autumn, and the winter of
life as perfect expressions...

then I, too, may grow.

— Ella Wheeler Wilcox

True wisdom is to be: always
seasonable, and to change
with a good grace in changing
circumstances.

— Robert Louis Stevenson

The Gift of Keeping
Young at Heart

Genius is childhood recaptured.

— Charles Baudelaire

It is familiarity with life that makes time
speed quickly. When every day is a step
into the unknown, as it is for children,
the days are long with the gathering
of experience.

— George Gissing

I am not young enough
to know everything.

— Sir James M. Barrie

I think it would help if every now and then
I let the child that shines within me
live in harmony with the adult
I'm required to be.

— Douglas Pagels

The Gift of Knowing that the Joy Is in the Journey

All life is an experiment. The more experiments you make, the better.

— Ralph Waldo Emerson

The truth is that it is natural,
as well as necessary, for every
man to be a vagabond occasionally.

— Samuel H. Hammond

This is a magnificent journey you're on.
Don't be afraid to explore unfamiliar
territory. If you do happen to get lost,
you will stumble across some of the
most interesting discoveries you will
ever make.

Wander down roads you've never explored
before and ones you'll never chance upon
again. Life isn't a travel guide to follow.
It's an adventure to undertake.

— Douglas Pagels

The Gift of Lighting
Candles in the Lives of Others

If one life shines, the life next to it
will catch the light.

— Anonymous

Go out of your way to be good to an older person.
You'll discover that you can make somebody's entire
day with a smile, a phone call, some fresh-picked
daisies, or whatever it is you've got.

Our elders have so much to give to those who listen,
but they are the ones who deserve to receive. Don't
pass up the chance to brighten their lives. An old
adage reminds us that they need only a little, but
they need that little — a lot.

— Douglas Pagels

It was only a glad "good morning"
As she passed along the way,
But it spread the morning's glory
Over the livelong day.

— Anonymous

The Gift of Living in
a More Forgiving World

As long as the world keeps spinning around,
none of its inhabitants will *ever* be able to raise
themselves up — by putting other people down.

— Douglas Pagels

Bigotry and intolerance are always the inevitable earmarks
of ignorance... while the results of education are sympathy
and understanding. To talk about education without
compassion is like talking about a crooked straight line.

— D. J. Sizoo

Wherever there is a human being, I see
God-given rights inherent in that being,
whatever may be the sex or complexion.

— William Lloyd Garrison

Every person, in whatever garb, or of whatever
station or origin, is deserving of a full need of
consideration and understanding. To determine
that everyone we meet receives from us a just
measure of civility is a worthy ambition and practice.

— Anonymous

The Gift of an Affinity
for the Environment

Heaven is under our feet,
as well as over our heads.

— Henry David Thoreau

Do your part for the planet. Do all the things
you know you "should" do. Our grandchildren's
children will either have words of praise for our
efforts and our foresight, or words that condemn
us for forgetting that they must live here long after
we are gone. Don't overlook the obvious: This is
not a dress rehearsal. This is the real thing. Our
presence has an impact, but our precautions do,
too. And the environment means the world to us.

— Douglas Pagels

Stoop and touch the earth, and receive its influence;
touch the flower, and feel its life; face the wind, and
have its meaning; let the sunlight fall on the open hand
as if you could hold it. Something may be grasped from
them all, invisible yet strong. It is the sense of a wider
existence — wider and higher.

— Richard Jefferies

The Gift of Using Pride as a Guiding Light

It is the greatest of advantages
to enjoy no advantage at all.

— Henry David Thoreau

To really know what success means,
earn it. Don't rely on some elevator
to take you there. The easiest lessons
to remember are the ones you learn
the hard way. The higher the floor
you want to reach, the more important
it is to take the stairs.

— Douglas Pagels

Worthy things happen
to the worthy.

— Plautus

Do the thing that is right
even when the boss isn't looking,
because the boss isn't a criterion.

The real boss is standing alongside you
every moment of your life.

— Alfred P. Haake

The Gift of a Lifetime
of Learning

The best kind of learning curve
is an educated smile.

— Douglas Pagels

It isn't how little you know that matters,
but how anxious you are to learn.

— C. Newland

Learning is like rowing upstream:
not to advance is to drop back.

— Chinese Proverb

The one who graduates today
and stops learning tomorrow
is uneducated the day after.

— Anonymous

If we are wise, we never leave school.

— Horace Fletcher

The Gift of Encouraging
a Child's Smile

Every... child on this earth has an overwhelming
desire to be loved, to be wanted, to be appreciated.
To the extent that we can fulfill this desire... will
we find happiness ourselves.

— Anonymous

Let the children be happy. Teach them to fill their hearts
with feelings of wonder and to be full of courage and hope.
Nothing is more important than the sharing of this moment
in time. Hold their kite strings, make their hearts sing, make
their smiles shine.

Reflect their inner and outer beauty. Encourage them to be
in less of a hurry. Love them each fleeting second. Try to
have the patience of a saint, and the understanding of one,
too. Admire them. Inspire them. And tell them in untold ways
what they mean to you.

— Douglas Pagels

Mankind is always happy for having been happy;
so that if you make them happy now, you make them
happy twenty years hence by the memory of it.

— Sydney Smith

The Gift of Controlling Your Own Destiny

If you think you can, or think you can't, you're probably right.

— Mark Twain

Clear your mind of can't.

— Samuel Johnson

The difference between perseverance and obstinacy is that one is motivated by a strong will, and the other by a strong won't.

— Anonymous

We can always do more and be more than we think we can. Let's *think* less and *imagine* more.

— Douglas Pagels

The Gift of Knowing that Health Is True Wealth

Take care of yourself. Good health
is everyone's major source of wealth.

— Anonymous

If your pursuit of wealth causes you to
sacrifice any aspect of your health, your
priorities are turned around.

Your physical condition is your compass;
it will tell you if you are headed in the right
direction or if you're going astray. It's not
your checkbook, but *you* who is counted
on to be there for the people in your world.
Be farsighted. Weigh the differences. Think
of the prices to pay.

— Douglas Pagels

One way to live happily ever after
is not to be after too much.

— Anonymous

The Gift of a More Peaceful World

Give me the money that has been spent in
war and I will clothe every man, woman, and
child in an attire of which kings and queens
will be proud. I will build a schoolhouse in
every valley over the whole earth. I will crown
every hillside with a place of worship
consecrated to peace.

— Charles Sumner

The more you're bothered by something that's wrong,
the more you're empowered to change things and make
them right. The more we follow that philosophy as
individuals, the easier it will be to brighten our horizons
outward from there, taking in our communities, our
cultures, our countries, and the common ground we
stand on.

The crucible of peace and good will is far too empty,
and each of us must — in some way — help to fill it.

— Douglas Pagels

We must be the change we wish to see in the world.

— Mohandas K. Gandhi

The Gift of Acquired Wisdom

If second thoughts came
before first thoughts, how
much wiser we would be.

— Anonymous

Life would be infinitely happier if we
could only be born at the age of 80
and gradually approach 18.

— Mark Twain

Life can only be understood backwards,
but it must be lived forwards.

— Sören Kierkegaard

What a fool does in the end,
a wise man does in the beginning.

— Spanish Proverb

The Gift of Learning
from Mistakes

Experience is a good teacher,
but she sends in terrific bills.

— Minna Antrim

Life continually teaches. We eventually
catch on. Some of us have master's degrees
in subjects we never intended to take. And
through our experiences, we realize: It's
okay to make mistakes. It's okay to fall.
It's a form of higher education.

— Douglas Pagels

If you don't learn from your mistakes,
there's no sense making them.

— Anonymous

The Gift of Rising Up
to Meet Your Potential

If we can put a man on the moon,
you can see your way through
to where you want to be.
There is a way.
There is *always* a way.

— Douglas Pagels

Have the daring to accept yourself as
a bundle of possibilities, and undertake
the game of making the most of your best.

— Harry Emerson Fosdick

No one knows what he can do
until he tries.

— Publilius Syrus

If we did all the things we are
capable of doing, we would
literally astound ourselves.

— Thomas A. Edison

The Gift of Allowing
for More Kindness

How beautiful a day can be
when kindness touches it!

— Anonymous

Do not stop with doing necessary kindnesses;
the unnecessary ones are of greater importance.

— Anonymous

Shall we make a new rule of life
from tonight: Always try to be a
little kinder than is necessary?

— Sir James M. Barrie

In this world, you must be a bit too kind
in order to be kind enough.

— Pierre Carlet de Chamblain de Marivaux

The Gift of Giving Yourself
Something Grand to Look Back On

The time will come when winter will
ask you what you were doing all summer.

— Henry Clay

Off in the distance, I see an old man sitting in a comfortable chair beside an open fireplace. No, this is not a picture of my father, or grandfather, facing life's sunset — it is myself.

I have decided now, in my days of prime, to be kind to that old man.... I am going to be kinder to the body he will have to use.... I am going to be more kind to the mind the old man will have to use. Like my body, I will try to keep it agile. It is said that old folks live in the past. I have resolved to give the old man some pleasant memories, some pleasant scenes to gaze upon. I want him to be able to look back and see deeds of kindness done, cheer brought into lonely hearts. I want him to look back upon some outstanding achievement.

I want to give the old man a quiet confidence
in the future.

— Anonymous

Old age is like anything else. To succeed
at it, you've got to start young.

— Anonymous

The Gift of Making
Each Day a Masterpiece

A life well lived is simply a compilation
of days well spent.

— Douglas Pagels

Time can't take away anything that has
already been given: Your treasures from
days gone by are treasures still; your
most precious memories will always be.

We learn, as we go along, that happiness
is not one big, beautiful jewel we can
hold — or lose — in our hands. Each one
of us is an hourglass. And in the course
of our lives, we get to keep the diamonds
that come our way among the passing sands.

— Douglas Pagels

Today is big
with blessings.

— Mary Baker Eddy

The Gift of Realizing Your Dreams

Follow your hopes and dreams while you can. While the desire is burning. When the chance comes your way. Don't be a ship that stays in the harbor, never straying from its safety. Don't get tangled up with "maybe... maybe someday." Too many folks will tell you that if you spend your whole life waiting, "someday" arrives too little, too late.

Maybe it's already a little later than it seems. If you really want to do it, do it while you can.
    Be brave... and sail away on your dreams.

— Douglas Pagels

For the people who are always going to do things: The road to Success lies along the path of Decision, and up the hill of Endeavor, and across the bridge of Patience. The road to Defeat lies through the valley of Pretty Soon and the winding paths of Wait-a-While.

— Ella Wheeler Wilcox

The road to success is dotted with
many tempting parking places.

— Anonymous

There's no traffic jam on the extra mile.

— Anonymous

The Gift of Many
Happy Returns

The world is round, and the place
which may seem like the end
may also be only the beginning.

— Ivy Baker Priest

The game of life is a game of
boomerangs. Our thoughts, deeds,
and words return to us sooner or
later with astounding accuracy.

— Anonymous

Then give to the world
the best you know
And the best will come
back to you.

— Henry Wadsworth Longfellow

The Gift of Knowing that Beautiful Tomorrows Begin Today

Tomorrow is a beautiful road
that will take you right where
you want to go...

If you spend today walking away
from worry and moving toward
serenity; leaving behind conflict
and traveling toward solutions;
and parting with emptiness and
never giving up on your search
for fulfillment. If you can do
what works for you, your present
will be happier and your path will
be smoother. And best of all?

You'll be taking a step
into a beautiful future.

— Douglas Pagels

We shall not cease from exploration
And the end of all our exploring
Will be to arrive where we started
And know the place for the first time.

— T. S. Eliot

Author-Editor Profile

Douglas Pagels has been a favorite Blue
Mountain Arts writer for many years. His
philosophical sayings and sentiments on
friendship and love have been translated
into seven languages and shared with
millions of people worldwide in notecards,
calendars, and his previous books. He lives
in the mountains of Colorado with his wife
and two sons.